OLD RAIGER
AND OTHER VERSE

THE WORKS OF JOHN MASEFIELD

PLAYS

The Faithful
Good Friday
Tristan and Isolt
Easter
Melloney Holtspur
A King's Daughter
The Trial of Jesus
The Tragedy of Nan
The Coming of Christ
End and Beginning

POETRY

Dauber
The Daffodil Fields
Philip the King
Lollingdon Downs
A Poem and Two Plays
Reynard the Fox
Enslaved
Right Royal
Selected Poems (new edition)
King Cole
Old Raiger and Other Verse
Poems (collected)
Midsummer Night
Minnie Maylow's Story
A Tale of Troy
A Letter from Pontus
Gautama the Enlightened
Wonderings
Natalie Maisie and Pavilastukay
On the Hill
The Bluebells and Other Verse

FICTION

Sard Harker
Odtaa
The Midnight Folk
The Hawbucks
The Bird of Dawning
The Taking of the Gry
The Box of Delights
Victorious Troy
Eggs and Baker
The Square Peg
Dead Ned
Live and Kicking Ned
Basilissa
Conquer

GENERAL

Gallipoli
The Old Front Line
St. George and the Dragon
The Battle of the Somme
Recent Prose
With the Living Voice
The Wanderer of Liverpool
Poetry: A Lecture
So Long to Learn
The Conway
The Nine Days Wonder
In the Mill
New Chum
Thanks Before Going and A Macbeth Production
A Book of Both Sorts
A Book of Prose Selections
William Shakespeare

JOHN MASEFIELD

*

OLD RAIGER

AND OTHER VERSE

THE MACMILLAN COMPANY
New York

First published 1965

Library of Congress Catalogue Number 65-12905

Printed in Great Britain

CONTENTS

THE SNIPE AT DRUM

Once, when the snipe were drumming,
When early bees were humming,
When radiant May was coming,
And cuckoos come,
That Mother, back beside us
Had come from Death to guide us,
Renewing love that tied us,
It seemed, to some.

So fresh the tasty buds were,
The young green hawthorn studs were,
So golden in the muds were
The cups of marigold,
So sure, each treasure-trover,
To find a four-leaf clover,
That winter all seemed over
And naught in Nature old.

The brook sang to the clover,
'This England ends at Dover,
So on, and be a rover,
For roving is a joy,
And youth, my lad's, a drover
Will lift you, the world over.'

Thus sang she, to the clover,
So thrilled she, to the boy.

OLD RAIGER

Prologue:

Good Old Man Raiger, raging in his rage,
He raged to rights, considering his age.
He was a cough-drop, raging, as all said,
A rage like his would strike a tombstone dead.
When he was raging under Wood Top Hill,
Old Parson trembled and the chimes stood still,
He sent his rage afore, Old Raiger done.
He scared 'em stiff, one son and t'other son.

This raging Raiger, who and what was he?
A widower, with Tom and Charles his sons,
Owning some land and having ships at sea.
The two sons, not yet wed,
The younger having heart, the elder head,
In quarrel, not at daggers drawn, but guns.

Tom, heir and elder, still in some disgrace,
For some low love-affair, out eastward way,
Now sought to oust his brother from the place
Courting the girl Charles wooed.
Charles was a bailiff altogether good.
The loved-one was the county beauty, May.

One of old Raiger's ships was due to sail,
On a time-charter, from the port near by.
Successions of small crosses turned the scale,
She missed her tide and stayed.
The message (telling Raiger) was delayed.
He heard of stoppage, not the reasons why.

Thinking at once, 'The charter may be lost',
(Two days already had been stricken null),
His fury sought for someone to be tosst.
The household heard his cries
Cursing his Captain's being, lungs and eyes,
The ship, her charter, mates and crew and hull.

Trembling, they heard Old Raiger leave his room,
Calling his sons to have the carriage brought;
He bellowed like the trumpeting of doom,
But neither son replied.
So, raging to their door, he flung it wide;
There, rolling on the floor, the brothers fought.

Tom, the beneath one, gasped, 'I am the heir,
'You're just an unpaid bailiff to the Farm.'
Charles said, 'I'll teach you, here or anywhere.
'You shall not trouble May.
'Marry your baggage there, out Pightle way.'
Then tooth and nail replied to knee and arm.

Old Raiger tore the two apart, and sent
Each, as he bid; and when they brought the chaise,
Mounting, he asked them what their fury meant,

Fighting like two mad curs.
'I'll disinherit both if this recurs,
Mark that, you dogs' . . . and galloped off ablaze.

But, soon as he had gone, the angry two
Were at each other's throats upon the floor
Seeking the answer which of them should woo
The lovely dark-haired May;
Tom cried, 'We'll settle this at break of day.
'Tomorrow, up at Wood Top, half past four.'

'Right,' Charles agreed. 'Rook-rifles, twenty paces,
'We'll walk apart, then turn; let lead decide.
'May shall not have to suffer your disgraces.
'Our rifles are a pair.'
Tom answered, 'Dawn tomorrow: I'll be there
'And lead shall settle . . . Wood-Top-covert-side.'

Some little grief for brotherhood of old
Was with them both at moments in the night . . .
Charles wakened early in the April cold
A little before day.
He took his gun and went the woodland way
In dripping dew and the beginning light.

There, upon Wood Top, Brother Tom was waiting,
Nursing his gun, with his back turned to him,
The blackbirds cackled for the night abating,
And now, as Charles drew near,
The figure turned, and struck him dumb with fear:
It was not Tom, but Raiger, mad and grim . . .

Mad beyond speech, but no one could mistake
The wordless rage, the fury of command,
The hell-fire tempest, just about to break,
His childhood's utmost dread.
Charles quailed and shrank although no word was said;
He backed, obedient to the pointed hand.

He backed before the fury to the gate,
Terrified, as in childhood, like a hound
Suddenly sick with terror at a rate,
Crouched to the lifted whip. . . .
But what had brought the Raiger from the ship?
How had he learned of duel, time and ground?

He shrank along the border of the wood,
Back, through the swing-gate, in among the scrubs,
Terrified still, but in the ride he stood,
To plead his desperate case.
In childhood, truth had often won him grace,
The old dog barked but didn't bite his cubs.

But this time, 'No,' he thought, 'No pardon, now.
'This is detection in a plotted crime . . .
'He has discovered it, I marvel how . . .
'This ruins both of us. . . .
'I've seen him rage of old, but never thus . . .
'And now we're ruined to the end of time.'

A minute passed, but Raiger did not come . . .
No sound of footsteps came from Wood Top field,
The rage of outraged fatherhood was dumb . .

'He's had a stroke,' Charles thought . . .
'Father,' he cried; but Father answered naught.
A rabbit's hopping paused, a blue jay squealed.

'Father,' he cried again. No Father followed.
This was unlike the Raiger when ablaze.
His furies ravened when his devil holloaed.
'Father, I'm here,' Charles cried.
'He's had a stroke,' he said, as none replied.
He ran to see, but lo, to his amaze . . .

No human being showed, alive or dead;
The mighty paleness of the Wood Top bare
Was desolate, save where a rabbit sped.
Of Raiger, no trace, none. . . .
Where he had raged was nothing but Tom's gun,
Tom's very gun and Tom's own footprints there.

There in the dew, where Raiger's shape had glared,
None but Tom's footprints darkened in the dew.
Now with another terror Charles was scared:
'But I saw Father here . . . .
'It was himself, and he is dead, I fear . . .
'Dead at our duel that he somehow knew . . .'

Taking Tom's gun, he said, 'We are accurst' . . .
– When, lo, there in the dew, was Jill, the maid,
Crying, 'O Master Charles, before the worst,
'Come quick, before he dies . . . .
'For Master Tom, at home, a-dying lies . . .
'He came in dying, like his wits were strayed.'

They raced for home, and there was Tom in bed,
Saying, 'I took my gun, and Father came,
'Speechless with anger, Charles, a thing of dread,
'A bombshell blazing bright . . .
'I am the wicked one, and you're the right . . .
'Soon he'll be here, Charles, and he'll strike us dead.'

'No, no,' Charles said. 'Shake hands, and let's be friends.'
The hands were shaken and the feud was done.
'Where did you see him, Tom?' 'At Wood Top Ends,
'Where I was waiting you.
'Lord knows how he discovered, but he knew,
'I ran for home and flung away my gun.'

'I have your gun,' Charles said, 'And Father's rage
'Is nothing now – our quarrel's set aside. . . .
'When he has blown his blast, he will assuage,
'Lie quiet and let be . . .
'I'll find him, Tom, – he never bothers me.'
But in his heart he thought, 'Father has died.

'Somehow, in death, he knew what we had planned
'And fury at our folly dealt the stroke . . . .
'And he the justest spirit in the land,
'Raging beyond all bounds,
'Panted to cudgel his two crazy hounds,
'And in the agony his great heart broke.

'That was his spirit sent for us to see
'To terrify and keep us from a crime.'
'Now, Tom,' he said, 'let bitter bygones be,

'All will be well . . . I'll out . . .
'I shall have news of Father without doubt.
'And food's a stand-by in a troublous time.'

So, rousing Tom from bed, and ordering food,
He went to ask had any seen or heard
Of Raiger back at home, in field or wood,
Or inns where mail-teams change. . . .
No one had news, all thought the question strange;
He hurried back to Tom without a word.

But news was coming, to make all alive;
While Tom and Charles took breakfast as of old,
A pair of grays came smoking up the drive,
It was The Game-Cocks' team.
Someone was coming thither in a steam,
Crunching the gravel, scattering the mould.

'Here's Father, then,' the Brothers spoke as one;
They heard an oath: the door was opened wide.
'Ha,' roared the Raiger, 'so the quarrel's done.
'I thought you two mad goats
'Had taken knives and cut each other's throats.
'Go, May's without; don't let her stay outside.'

They brought a blushing May: they offered chairs.
All trembled as the Raiger drew his breath;
He froze the Brothers with ferocious glares.
'You two blind jangling jays . . .
'You've nearly killed me with your crazy ways.
'But, Sirs, I'll stop your folly before death.

‘Give me some coffee, May . . . the foes are friends,
‘For all my gallop in the dark, they’re cool.
‘But hark ’ee, Masters, this your quarrel ends.
‘You cocks, red in the comb,
‘Will keep this not a cockpit but a home.
‘I stand no nonsense more from either fool.

‘No more such madness. Firstly, Tom the heir.
‘Your girl, out at the Earls, is married now,
‘The Pightle Inn man’s wedded to her there.
‘It must be understood
‘That all that rotten gossip stops for good:
‘The matter ends, I care not why nor how.

‘You’ll leave her there, whatever may have been,
‘Of young man’s folly or of woman’s lies.
‘Take it from me, you’ll marry as I mean . . .
‘Jemima . . . understand.
‘You’ll go today to ask her for her hand.
‘You’ll link the two estates, Sir: so be wise.

‘I met Jemima’s father, coming here.
‘Your marriage with Jemima is arranged
‘(All but the wedding-day and ringers’ beer).
‘I know you like the lass.
‘(A cut above you, too, but let that pass . . .
‘The glass has risen and the wind has changed.)

‘Now, lovely May, daughter of my old friend,
‘Forgive these fore-words; now I come to you . . .
‘Men make the ruins that the women mend.

'This ruin here of ours,
'With you, may soon be beautiful with flowers;
'Charles isn't much, but can be made to do.

'Now, Charles, you don't deserve, but will, in time;
'I know you love this sweet beloved Spring,
'You'd marry her, but haven't got a dime.
'Now the Home Farm is yours.
'Whatever follies happen, land endures;
'Ask her, arrange the banns, and buy the ring.'

He rose and thrust Charles down upon his knees.
There at May's feet, and May was not unkind.
Tom blushed and paled and shuffled, ill at ease.
'Sir,' he said, 'Sir, forgive . . . .
'We three are pledged to friendship while we live.
'By tea-time I will know Jemima's mind.'

'Good,' said Old Raiger. 'Now, my bantam cocks,
'Eat . . . then I'll sleep . . . I've had a wearing night.
'The charter's safe, apart from Ocean's knocks . . .
'No need to call me hence.
'But suddenly I had a shocking sense
'That you two crazy bull-calves meant to fight.

'Duel, in fact, at dawn, beyond the wood . . .
'(I was at Docks, with thirty miles to go)
'I swore I'd stop your folly if I could . . .
'So off, with a fresh team.
'Clear roads and moonlight we could put on steam.
' "Those fools,' I said, 'I'll stop their folly, though.' "

'Mind, it was not impossible to do,
'I thought we'd do it, but we met delays . . .
'Slowing for sloughs, and casting of a shoe,
'And ostlers all asleep,
'Myself, all mad at you two silly sheep,
'All dynamite, exploding into blaze.

'But morning caught me, as I might have known
'At Scrobbles (Squire's Gate) you know the place,
'And there stood Squire waiting all alone
'The Morning Mail to town.
'It seemed insanity, but I got down
'And settled with him in Jemima's case.

' "Crazy," you'll say, "to settle Tom's affair.
' "Just when already (haply) Charles and he
' "Had blown their silly ghosts into the air."
'Yes . . . but I next fetched May,
'She might be having a most tragic day,
'And where was comfort for her, save in me?

'By George, you two have given me a dance,
'And all for nothing, for you've made a peace,
'And tragedy collapses in romance.
'Now, I'll to bed to rest.
'Tom, off to see Jemima, it were best.
'Charles, tip the driver till the horses prance.'

Epilogue:

That's what the tale says Raging Raiger did
To stop his sons from doing what's forbid.
Finding he couldn't get to 'em, he sent
His spirit from him, and his spirit went
And scared 'em proper out of their two skins.
A terror will work wonder against sins.

He stopped them doing murder, that's a fact;
And stopping murder is a righteous act.
Many (as disliked Raiger) would admit
The old dog came with credit out of it.

But the two wild-cat boys got wives of sense.
Jemima brought th' estates into one fence,
And some (as disliked Raiger) sorrowed sore
To know he'd got the grass he lusted for,
Old Butter Pastures, that he'd longed-for long.

Raiger, if you'll permit me, he was strong.
Not in weight-lifting, nor in pitching hay,
But bowing all things down to have his way.
You wouldn't think it, not to see him, quite;
He never fought, he never had to fight.

But what he had in mind he had in mill,
Grinding all cross-conclusions to his will.
Maybe for thirty years his will was burning,

And all the thirty years the lane was turning.
'Nothing turns lanes, but will,' Old Raiger said. . . .

'Willing a thing, and knowing how to wait,
'And passing time, make many crookeds straight.
'But Willing is the Boy,' Old Raiger said.

A many sorrowed for Old Raiger dead.

THE ALONG-SHIPS STOW

Treacle, treacle, little ship,
Hither, mariners, and sip,
Buckets, mariners, and dip.

I was the Second in the *Captain Bold*,
Bound north, with general freight, from
Port of Peace,
Myself the very youth, the ship was old;
And leaving port, the wind on the increase,
I, fresh to berth and ship,
Knew from the dances she began to skip
That if she had a fault, it was, she rolled.

And as the gale increased, I thought the more
About the casked molasses we had stowed,
Up to the hatches there at Sugar-Shore . . .
A danger-freight for any ship to load.
I had stowed thwart-ship tiers . . .
Then the old mate had come about my ears
Swearing along-ships was the proper mode.

Well, seniors order, second mates endure,
Molasses tests the methods and decides;
The weather would be wicked, that was sure,
In wicked weather nothing wrong abides.

Things worsened, the glass fell;
The squallings stiffened into steady yell,
The forward well-deck often took it pure.

At first the rainfall kept the sea in check,
As rainfall will, but as the day went by,
Men needed life-lines on the open deck.
Then, what seemed smoke came skimming over sky . . .
Galloping smoke at first,
Then blackness, wilderness and thunder-burst,
And sea-hounds crying for a ship to wreck.

Well . . . as it worsened, nothing could be done
But lay her by and listen while it raved.
The Old Man shouted, 'Mister . . . listen, son . . .
'Find if those 'tweendeck casks are getting staved.
'It's certain to blow worse.
'Molasses in a cargo is a curse.
'Before it lulls, she'll stave a hundred ton.'

So down I went in semi-dark, and clung,
Under a man-hole peering to observe,
My feet jammed on the uprights of the rung,
My body bracing to her heave and swerve.
I saw a great grim cave
Where every inch a moaning whimper gave
For every inch was hurt and giving tongue.

Within the stifling tumult of the cave,
Along the 'long-ship-tiers the Mate had stowed,
Barrel on barrel had begun to stave,

And others strained to travel the same road.
The treacle struggled through
The started staves in seepages of glue
Which pressed, and, bursting bonds, became a wave.

Everywhere, treacle-tear and treacle-drip,
Staves, bungs and dunnage whelmed in a thick heave,
Dense treacle feelers getting a good grip;
I cannot tell it, nor can you believe . . .
Slow-loitering, surging swift
According to the plunging or the lift
Of the tormented, (haply dying) ship.

Below, the 'long-ship-tiers my thwart-ships stow
Still stood the strain (so far as I could see).
The truth about them nobody could know
But they were standing as it seemed to me.
As for 'a hundred ton',
The Old Man's guess, I reckoned every one
Was doomed to perish; all the lot would go.

Aghast, I watched the treacle as it oozed,
As roll or squatter made the barrels grind
Beyond the competence of things ill-used . . .
I cannot lose the picture from my mind . . .
The 'tweendecks of an ark
Hot, screaming dimness suddenly made dark
For suddenly the 'tweendecks lighting fused.

Straight, I reported that the 'tweendeck stow
Was staving, piece-meal, as it seemed to me.

A hundred casks had gone and more would go,
Destroyed between the devil and the sea.
'It must just take its way,'
The Old Man said, 'and if it spills, it may.
'We cannot trim it till it stops to blow.'

So there we rolled, and took it green, and lay,
In a great roaring in a sea gone mad,
Unknowing whether it were rain or spray
That drenched us in the sousings that we had.
The Chief sent up to tell,
'A lot of treacle's got into the well.'
'Then pump and clear the muck', we sent to say.

The pumps began, but as the proverb tells,
'The blow comes on the bruise', and so with us.
Things worse than treacle get in pumps and wells,
Rupture and wreck and cloggings ruinous.
We felt the pump-throb beat,
Thumping the planking underneath our feet,
Suddenly stop, and stay stopped, 'twixt two bells.

'What stops the pump?' the Old Man said to me,
'Go down and find . . . and how's the treacle there?
'The Devil's always where he shouldn't be,
'And treacle is a devil everywhere.'
Below, I was appalled
To find a stokehold floor where treacle crawled,
A teatime tide out of a soupy sea.

I trod in treacle over my boot's sole,
Treacle was oozing out of chinks and seams.

Some pump-repairers, crouched against the roll,
Sweated in heat beyond the devil's dreams.
They fingered filth and curst.
One of them said, 'Then it's the sprangle burst . . .
'It's only treacle, this, with bits of coal.'

I asked the Second, when the leak began.
He answered: 'Find out, if you want to know.
'This hooker is an obsolete tin can,
'Fit for the knackers twenty years ago.
'She's rolled her fixings loose,
'And what we tread in is her vital juice.
'Report it, with our love, to the Old Man.'

The Old Man said, 'You know that treacle burns,
'And what may come at sea one never knows.
'Man never knows the ocean, but he learns,
'You'll learn where treacle gets to when it flows.
'If it should reach the fires,
'This ship will be a sight as she expires,
'This morning in the Bay of No-Returns.

'To burn in treacle isn't to my mind,
'Somehow a lot of it has found its way . . .
'Whatever way it comes, the rest will find
'And we must bale it till the pump can play.
'By all I can observe,
'This storm is making her Atlantic swerve,
'We'll see a star (or Heaven) before day.

'Go, muster every bucket, scoop and broom
'And bale the stuff and dump it as she dips.'

I took the watch into the engine-room,
And we and treacle fairly came to grips.
We scraped what wouldn't yield,
We poured what wouldn't empty as she heeled,
And this in tropic heat and treacle-drips.

At first, when we were fresh, new to the toil,
Glad of the chance of something to be done,
More than just holding on and dripping oil,
We formed the bucket-chain and thought it fun.
Then when fatigue began,
I tried a song, as when a shanty-man
Bids halliard-haulers stretch along the coil.

'O treacle is the life of man,
'Treacle. Jemima.
'O treacle is the life of man,
'Treacle for Jemima.

'I scoop it up in an old tin pan,
'Treacle. Jemima.
'I scoop it up in an old tin pan,
'Treacle for Jemima.'

And as we shantied, stuck with treacle and sweat,
I heard a stoker grubbing in the pipes
Growl, 'Why, they haven't tried the sprangle yet . . .
'The sprangle's bust and tore the dick to stripes.'
The Chief replied, all-glowing:
'While you're aboard here, keep your clock from going.
'Springle your sprangles elsewhere . . . don't forget.'

Indeed, the strain had made all bearings hot.
The chorus failed, the shanty-singing died.
It made a fellow's very heart-blood clot
To get one bucketful tipped overside.
Then, suddenly, a flood
Of treacle hideous as an ogre's blood
Surged from a dozen barrels gone to pot.

Just on despair-point the disaster fell.
'Together, boys', we cried, and all together
We grappled with that new attack from hell,
All gasping at the ending of our tether.
Against Death's self we baled;
The stuff would reach the fires if we failed.
And failure neared, as any fool could tell.

And then the Old Man with his steward came,
Hot coffee mixed with rum, a mugful each:
A respite in the crisis of the game,
Life in the rum and comfort in the speech.
'By all I can observe,
'This storm has taken her Atlantic swerve.
'It blows like Barney's Bull, though, all the same.'

But with the strength thus given we returned
To bucket up the surgings of the gum
And still the rolling hooker plunged and churned
And pitched us, man and bucket, in the scum.
And still, in the black pit,
The engineers still struggled to re-fit
The thing without which we might all be burned.

Sea-knowledge knows that when the glasses rise
The strongest winds come, and the seas are worst;
Then comes the moment when the hooker dies,
Propellers drop away and hatches burst.
That very worst we felt;
Down went the swearing searchers as they knelt,
The treacle took us, as a gum takes flies.

We slithered all to leeward where we lay,
Heaped in a jam from one appalling blast.
I thought 'Here endeth; this is Judgment Day,
'She'll never weather this . . . this is the last.'
She lay beam-ended, thrust
By one long roar of never-ending gust,
Such as puts shipping into Dead Man's Bay.

How long she cowered I shall never know
But after a long age, slowly, she crawled
Into a weather-roll, but O so slow . . .
I wondered still . . . and then, I was appalled:
As she rolled back I saw
Molasses in a tidal wave of awe,
All the last barrels of the 'long-ships stow.

A stoker cried, 'It *was* the sprangle, then.'
The sprangle didn't move me: treacle did.
I called, 'Together, now . . . Up buckets, men.'
Slowly they formed the chain on being bid,
In treacle a foot deep,
Their eyes all treacle, strain and want of sleep,
I hope never to see the like agen.

But now the game was up, the treacle gained,
The hands worn out, and no relief remaining,
Dogged and dripping, done and over-strained,
The weather worse, the treacle ever gaining.
'No, not another turn,'
The leader said at last. 'We'll have to burn.'
Out of a new seam spurts of treacle rained

'Come, boys, it's bale or broil,' I said, but no,
They were good men, but finished; they were done.
It was so odd to see the buckets go,
Flop in the treacle there from everyone.
And then to see them float
As the ship rolled, each like a listed boat.
Mind, it was light now, morning had begun.

'We're done, sir,' a man said, 'we're beaten out.
'Not one of us can do another turn.
'Our number's up and fortune's up the spout.
'And if it's burn or baling, we must burn.'
I said, 'Wait till I come . . .
'Spell-O a while . . . I'll muster for some rum.
'Another lively spell may end the bout.'

Just as I seized the iron rail to climb
Men fitted a new sprangle in the dim.
The treacly engineers all black with grime
Made the pump chug and started on a hymn.
She chugged with steady thrill . . .
All hands again upped buckets with a will,
It was just Christmas-time and Easter-time.

And then, with clearing squalls, it ceased to blow,
The tropic sunlight burned, the sea went down,
Soon we had revelled in a watch below,
Soon we were clean and smartened up for town,
How Peace dissolves ill spells.
Saint Nicholas' and Woodside Ferry bells
Made all that treacled night seem long ago.

RYEMEADOWS

My people owned Ryemeadows on the Moor,
There I was born, and there I hope to die,
Though, as the name suggests, the land is poor:
Scant arable, thin grazing and the sky:
Those and the moorland in its desolation
Marked here and there with dwellings of men past
Where men may meet what makes the soul aghast.

Mighty, the moor is: to the very small
Such as myself its greatness terrified;
Too soon I learned that it was feared by all,
Being the haunt of scoundrels who had died.
Murderers hanged in chains in expiation
Of bloodshed on the moor, who did not die
But climbed down from their chains to terrify . . .

These, and some other wicked ones, and worse,
Who moved at midnight doing evil still.
The mail-coach full of corpses like a hearse,
With that grim guard who made the blood run chill
Who hailed the midnight rover with temptation:
'Step in, Sir, for the inn at Dead Man's Bay,
'Cool going, quiet beds and naught to pay.'

Terrible tales, that made the blood run cold,
But not the worst, for these, they said, obeyed

The righteous heart and did what they were told,
Or could, by parish priest, be truly laid.
What scared me worse were stories of a Nation
Seldseen, unholy, vexing human lives,
Stealing men's children, or new-married wives.

'They were revengeful', people said, 'unkind . . .'
Dreadful to people if their wills were checked –
With spies abroad, to tell what men maligned,
And all maligners had their projects wrecked:
Wakened at night with screams of execration,
Pelted from markets or their cows made dry,
Or the year's cheeses such as none would buy.

These were the Fairy people who had danced
Those browner rings upon the scanty grazing,
Where Jane, our cook, had seen them as it chanced
Dancing in reels to pipings most amazing,
All bright with jewels in some celebration
For their great Queen, whose face Jane could not see;
She said, 'I looked into eternity'.

She said, 'It was vouchsafed: a something given,
'I know they are, but not in life like ours;
'If human life is hell, theirs is not Heaven;
'Men may have mind, the fairies other powers.
'They have no sin, no sorrow, no salvation,
'We have the two and struggle for the third.
'Leave them in quiet . . . not another word.'

So not another word would come from Jane,
And she repented having told me this,

And I, in hope, again and yet again
Went where her eyes had seen these mysteries.
A tor-top near a wind-blown larch plantation,
There in a big ring brown upon the green
She had seen fairies dancing to their Queen.

And longing still to see them, I would read
All I could find, and pestered all about,
Asking if fairies lived, in very deed.
The elders answered, 'Yes, beyond all doubt',
And glanced behind them in some perturbation
And added, 'Yes . . but do not ask such things
'For walls have ears, remember, and ears, wings.'

Then I met Tom, a somewhat elder lad,
Who taught me break-backs with a ball, and chess,
What birds he knew, and all the eggs he had,
Mimicked the cries of rabbits in distress
To call out weasels to my admiration,
And showed me swallows teaching younger hands
The soon-used milestones into sunnier lands.

Tom disbelieved the tales, for older boys
Had called them false: 'Fairies do not exist.
'On market-nights men get all out of poise
'Coming home drunk at midnight through the mist.
'They lose their silly ways and have vexation
'Stuck in a bog or stumbled in a burn.
'Or get dumb-founded taking a wrong turn.

'Then, the next morning, seven miles from home,
'They say, "The fairies rid them, out of spite.

‘ “Puck or The Lubber or some other gnome
‘ “Led them bedevilled all the weary night.” ’
Thus the boys spoke, with mock and indignation,
To Tom, and Tom to me, and this their tune
Was my tune also until afternoon.

But then, as the sun wested, and I knew
That soon the Night, the Fairy time, would fall,
That murderers’ feet would sully the pure dew,
And the white shape glide slow by the church wall,
Why, then, what powers seeking expiation
From those who doubted fairies, might soon climb
Ryemeadows stairs to steal me for a time?

Ah, when the Night closed in, and an owl screamed,
When, in the roof, a death-watch beetle tapped,
When, on the staircase, stealthy footsteps seemed,
Or from the wall some creeper’s holding snapped,
Or if a distant dog in desperation
(Left waterless perhaps) raved in his crying,
And all things told that Death came, for one dying:

Ah, then, indeed, I knew that the Night teemed
With evil powers many as a Nation,
More, and more awful than we mortals dreamed,
A loveless and inhuman generation
That from a midnight kingdom somehow streamed
Out from a nowhere never seen nor mapped
To hurry human beings to damnation.

JANE

In June time once, as I was going
Up Happen Hill, by Lobs's Pound,
I saw THEM, many as snow snowing,
Hymning their Queen and dancing round.

In glitter and sparkle they were turning,
Scattering dewdrops in the green,
Their jewels shone, their eyes were burning,
And O the Beauty of their Queen.

And O the beauty of their singing,
It was as beautiful as She,
Perfect in tune, in time, and bringing
A deathlessness to mortal me.

So Life, I knew, has this for kernel,
This marvel, to which man is blind:
We make a blur round an Eternal
For ever shaming humankind.

They streamed away, away, before me,
With chimes like little silver bells,
They opened doors of glory for me,
And now I think of nothing else.

PAWN TO BISHOP'S FIVE

I stayed, once, at Tom's home, at Uppats Lea,
In a green valley, where a brook rejoiced,
The happiest place wherein a boy could be,
In the first sun, in April, many-voiced.
I had played chess with Tom out of a book,
In which a master, in a champion's game,
Played Pawn to Bishop's Five, and overcame . . .
And all the great attack was clear to me.

Tom had some other task, I was alone,
I wandered to the brook, seeing the board
With all the pieces into vision grown,
Making the seven moves till Mate was scored.
Pawn, zig-zag Knight, sectarian Bishop, Rook,
Alive in me, and well-remembered yet.
Youth may attain what age cannot forget . . .
I crossed the brook, hopping from stone to stone.

And being, then, in wood, went up the stream
That ran in shade, wide, shallow, brightly-falling
On many stones, with many a sunny gleam,
And ever hurrying on, and ever calling.
Lush, brittle alder sprays and bramble-thorn

Checked my adventure, but I held my course,
Saying, 'I'll trace this water to its source.'
The chess-game filled my mind like a glad dream.

Most certainly, the wildness of the place
Showed that few people ever trod that wood.
Of pathway and of footprint were no trace,
The babbling water spoke to solitude.
With face and fingers scratched, and jacket torn,
I came out into moorland green and lone
Where the brook's being lipped over a stone,
Giving the spot an ecstasy of grace.

Though this was near, I somehow feared to tread
The slope to see from whence the water spilled.
Explorer's triumph overcame the dread . . .
I saw a shallow hollow, nearly filled
With water, trembling up from a stone floor.
And there, intently, in the April sun,
In water, among water-weed, was one,
Nay, two, playing with chessmen, white and red.

Spring's very self gave beauty to the pool;
A wild white cherry let her petals drip
Into the clearness, to go sailing cool
In wrinkling water, to the stony lip.
All April's gayest gems the selvage wore;
Primroses, violets, both white and blue,
Daisies, the best that ever fed on dew,
With all May's oxlips and her lady-smocks.

But O, the Indian Prince who played the chess:
The Spirit of the Brook, clear-eyed and proud,
Playing the Red men with a Chieftainess
Who played the White, over the water bowed,
The chessboard on a grassy stone between.
The Spirit of the Brook lounged half-submerged,
His latest move an utter crisis urged,
She, whom he played with, seemed oppressed and cowed.

Sure of his game, he waited, overbold,
Insolent, smiling, mocking her who played,
Yet having grace that never could grow old,
Lounged in the swaying cress his body swayed.
She turned as I approached: she was a Queen,
Queen of the violets, for blue and white
Violets made her raiment all delight.
He could not die, and she could never fade.

They saw me as not seeing, so I neared.
I was not terrified, but stricken dumb . . .
These were the fairies that so many feared,
And so few saw, myself the lucky some.
I crept nearer to see, perhaps to pray
To those small marvels so intensely live . . .
Was theirs the beauty to which souls arrive:
Perfected spirits, who have overcome?

And, staring down, I saw upon the board
The very game that so delighted me
Before the pawn's advancement drew the sword
And led the White attack to victory.

Though, still, the Princess doubted what to play,
She pondered, while her face, clear with bright thought,
In depth of wonder and of beauty wrought
As a young child's will, looking at the sea.

Yet, still, she wondered, while the Indian Prince
Mocked her delay, thinking the battle won:
His look I have remembered ever since,
While her dear spirit mustered, one by one,
The moves to turn the game a happier way.
And all my being burned into intense
Dear love for her, to quell his insolence
And snap his self-conceited malison.

And, knowing all the game from that same pause,
The move that loosed White pieces to success
In swift and certain ruin of Red's cause,
My spirit burned the clue to the Princess:
'The Pawn to Bishop's Five'; the words so clear,
And the succeeding moves so fiery bright
They danced there, like a little stream of light,
Thought being light in all her higher laws.

'The Pawn to Bishop's Five' . . . and lo, she heard:
Or knew, and saw, and for an instant gazed
With thanks into my face without a word.
The beauty of her thanking left me dazed,
It was so sweet, so exquisitely dear,
Herself so beautiful past power to tell.
She played the pawn at once, and the blow fell.
The mocker with the Red men ceased to gird.

His dark face blenched with fury, his hand crushed
A captured Bishop into coral grits,
And flung them where the current strongly gushed;
Like little scarlet raindrops fell the bits.
He said: 'You mate in seven moves: it's clear . . .
'These mortals who come treading everywhere . . .
'Let them, in future, tremble and beware
'Of tempest in their blood, storm in their wits.'

He beat his hand upon the board, that broke;
The pieces vanished, he himself was gone,
The princess faded like a tiny smoke.
The water trembled up and eddied on,
Over the wet lip of the little weir.
No trace of chess or players, sound or sight,
Stayed in that water-garden of delight:
The weeds swayed, the brook babbled, the sun shone.

And I, much moved, returned another way,
And never told a soul what I had seen;
But marked the day as a red-letter day;
Had not my prompting helped a fairy queen?
Sometimes in certain spots I felt her near,
Thanking me once again with that shy look.
I kept away thenceforward from the brook.
The promised storm and tempest have not been.

WHEN APRIL COMES

'April awaits the bold', he said,
'April's a wondrous thing.
'He who can seize the time and place
'May kiss with April face to face
'And pass into the Spring.

'And live in Spring with her', he said,
'Consider, you, the prize . . .
'To breathe what makes the cuckoo-toll
'That startles love within the soul
'And wisdom in the wise.

'In every Spring of all', he said,
'One moment is supreme
'When Spring's divinest beauty spreads
'And shakes all hearts and turns all heads,
'Till Winter is a husk one sheds,
'And frost a dimming dream.

'That is the time to snatch', he said,
'When April will descend
'And take to mate a mortal one
'And make him planet to the Sun
'Till universes end.

‘So, every year I’m bold’, he said,
‘As soon as days are long,
‘When little rabbits are first born
‘And sallets green upon the thorn
‘And blackbirds are in song.

‘For then, the Impulse tells’, he said,
‘That April walks the wold . . .
‘With all Eternity to share,
‘So out I come to question where,
‘Intending to be bold.

‘But, mind, I’m crafty, too,’ he said,
‘I seek a guiding word . . .
‘I ask the vixen with her cubs
‘At Wicked Hill or Ghost Heath Stubs,
‘I ask her, “Has she heard . . .
‘ “Heard any word at all” ’, he said,
‘ “Where April means to be
‘ “This crescent-moon, or that great night
‘ “When the full moon will be one white,
‘ “White lamp in a white sea?’

‘But vixens are so coy’, he said,
‘And never prone to talk.
‘It’s best to ask the hedgehog wise,
‘The midnight one with gleamy eyes,
‘So stilty in his walk . . .

‘Or better still than he’, he said,
‘The one who floats the air . . .

'The one it's better not to name,
'The one we know not whence he came
'Who goes we know not where . . .

'But when it comes to him', he said,
'To him, and such as he,
'My hair stands up upon my head,
'My teeth go clatter-clack for dread
'And terror palsies me . . .

'So I keep clear of him', he said,
'It's wiser so to do . . .
'And what I do, I manage so
'That he can never, never know,
'But I can whisper you. . . .

'To Universal Door', he said,
'There must be many keys . . .
'Such as have no affair with him . . .
'The light that gives the glow-worm glim
'And shines in summer seas . . . .

'The blue of violets', he said,
'The scent of the wild rose
'The velvet of the primrose-leaves,
'The cry with which the curlew grieves,
'And others, such as those.

'But littler things than those', he said,
'By what the sages say. . . .
'The shrew mice know a thing or two;

'You mind the way they look at you
'Next ninth September day.

'But let September be', he said,
'For time and time again . . .
'Men say I'm draughty in the dome,
'That what I seek is Harvest-Home,
'And I must make it plain . . .

'It isn't Harvest-Home', he said,
'That I go search and seek. . . .
'For Harvest-Home let others care
'When pommace perfumes country air
'From apples red in cheek.

'And never, never think', he said,
'I speak in its dispraise.
'I love it and I ever will
'When golden corn goes down to mill,
'And geese grow fat at graze.

'It is a golden time', he said,
'When promise comes to fruit,
'It is a holy time that gives
'The only food of all that lives
'By earth and leaf and root. . . .

'But what I seek, and shall', he said,
'Is Spring that blows the blast
'That makes the daffodil so brave
'And frees Earth's spirit from the grave
'And tells that winter's past. . . .

'But many say BEWARE', he said,
'BEWARE THIS STATE OF MIND,
'Lest making friends with Nature's Queen
'Put Fire to a Magazine
'And murder all mankind.

'They tell all sorts of tales', he said,
'How wicked men of old,
'When seeking more than mortals ought,
'Were blasted suddenly to naught
'As dust upon the mould.

'But what they sought was Death', he said,
'The power to make hell;
'To grind mankind between two stones,
'To kill the life and sell the bones.
'The blast that blows such Devil's Owns,
'I say it blasts 'em well.

'I'm none of any such', he said,
'I seek a wondrous friend
'Whose being makes the winter done,
'Who, if I seem a righteous one,
'Will make me planet to the Sun,
'Till universes end.

'But what is difficult', he said,
'Is how folk disagree
'About the very instant when
'The April Queen comes down to men
'And when She'll come to me. . . .

‘Some say “Atween-time time” ’, he said,
‘The tiptoe time of year,
‘A knife-edge time, with cuckoo come
‘And nightingale, but both still dumb,
‘Until the Queen appear.

‘But that is plainly false’, he said,
‘Beyond all kind of doubt.
‘Why, madmen know that Spring begins
‘As soon as gold is on the whins
‘And honey-bees are out.

‘But where to look for Her’, he said,
‘That makes a fellow muse,
‘For April on her windy feet
‘Brings green to many fields of wheat,
‘And which am I to choose?

‘The only clue I’ve heard’, he said,
‘Is that she’ll choose a place
‘Where sweet white violets are found,
‘Beside a brook whose little sound
‘Gives out a special grace.

‘Now that, I feel, is true’, he said,
‘But where is never told . . .
‘But it will be in some such spot,
‘That those who know it tell it not,
‘And I am growing old.

‘But what is comforting’, he said,
‘Is that the Stars may plan . . .

'The Universe's Mind may stir
'To tell the Queen I'm seeking Her
'Although but mortal man.

'And what is certain is . . .', he said,
'That when She hears it, She
'Will say "By longing for the Sun
' "All everlasting things are won"
'And She will pity me.

'But what perplexes most', he said,
'Is this . . . suppose She come . . .
'And tries me with some magic word
'That needs replies I haven't heard . . .
'And leaves me stricken dumb?

'But I believe my heart', he said,
'And man's heart tells him true. . . .
'When Sun has gone and night is here
'And all is moonless, mad and drear,
'And not a star by which to steer,
  'It prompts you what to do . . .
  'The first thing, to have done with fear,
  'And speak what springs in you.

'So I am going on', he said.

MORNINGS AND APRILS

PART I

Before the Sun has risen,
The sky above is as a windless lake,
A dream, a dim, wherein no planets glisten,
No clouds, from any breath, their courses take.
The Dawn, with the annulling of the prison,
Sighs, as the leaves stir, 'O awake, awake . . .

'Wake, for the peacocks on the cedar-boughs
'Have called, and shaken wing.
'Upon the dovecot-perch, the tumblers rouse.
'Under the belfry, ringers, going to ring,
'Crunch on the gravel: in the waking House,
'Up- and down-stairs, candles are glimmering.'

Within the tower, ringers' fingers grope,
Each, for his pull; his foot strikes as he heaves.
The creak runs up the rope
Startling the jackdaws roosting in the eaves;
And clangings stumble into cries of Hope:
'Awake, though Danger threat and Death bereaves . . .

'Awake, for, from the never-pastured whins
'The Morning comes with all-refreshing dew,

'Light with her revelation re-begins;
'Will you not waken, too?
'There is no room in any of the inns
'For those whose singings may awaken you.

'Immeasurably vast the starry stage,
'Its guidances incomparably bright,
'Unutterably old the pilgrimage
'From unseen specks to spirits infinite.
'The iron-seeming cage
'Dissolves before the living show of might.

'Surely, a swallow has already told
'Of apple-blossom buds about to break;
'The curlews are in laughter as of old
'Above the reed-bed bordering the lake;
'In meadows early cowslips glisten gold;
'Shall not man's soul awake?'

PART II

Out of what nights of old
Has Morning quickened upon Earth's despair,
With ending of the peril and the cold,
And healing of the pain too great to bear?
Into what midnight has the planet rolled
Since planets roamed and lights and darkness were?

Forgotten by mankind, however vast,
Those darknesses and ills
By which Earth's fortunes once were overcast

Beyond all hope and help of living skills,
We find the scattered relics of the past
From ruins in the bonework of the hills.

Into immensities of death and dust
This planet of man's home has had to range,
While mile-deep glaciers thrust,
Grinding a passage for their wintry change;
Or powdered systems in their orbits' gust
Have covered sea and glacier, grass and grange.

Not only giant Death, but monster Birth
Has marked this planet as she swims the skies.
Monsters of murder throughout sea and earth
Have used Life's enterprise,
Tooth, talon, poison, filling fell and firth
With creatures, slaughter-cunning and unwise.

Monstrous in secrecies within the lake,
The armoured terrors of the water hid,
Waiting the evening beasts with thirsts to slake.
The silences of stripes of tigers glid
For some stag's back to break.
Like weeds in the green depths wavered the squid.

But scanty utterance of Life Earth knew
Save dying cries of creatures at an end
Or the cackle that some cock of murder crew.
Life was a millioned massacre unkenned,
Scattering blood on every morning's dew
As coin Life had to spend.

PART III

Men say, 'The ice recedes.
'The dinosaurs and sabre-teeth are gone;
'The monsters perished as unwanted weeds.
'To calmer times the planet wanders on,
'To ages peopled by illumined breeds
'From whom perfected life will spring anon.'

Until that Morning of Attainment show,
Let man recall and praise
Mornings that seemed to people long ago
Like cherry-blossom after winter days;
Mornings that in the memory leave a glow
As in heroic tales the thrill that stays.

Such were the Mornings when diseases stayed:
The plague, the spotted pestilence, or worse . . .
Swift death to man and maid;
Death beyond drug or doctor, knife or nurse;
Hundreds of dead in hurried trenches laid
Under some Sun's intolerable curse.

Mornings have lightened even such despair;
Mercy has come, a frost perhaps, or rain,
And suddenly the terror was not there.
The Life began again,
The Death withdrew into his secret lair,
The human Hope returned into the brain.

Then, in the Night of War, how many times,
In utter hopelessness, have people known

How slowly up the dark the daybreak climbs!
Even to these, at last, has dawning shown.
The doers of the crimes
Are as forgotten leaves that wind has blown.

Or in a battle-smoke, in sweat and mud,
When Victory has swung from side to side,
When both the maddened armies were in flood
Spilling their lives, that Fortune might decide,
Some sudden gleam has thrilled in quickened blood,
And Morning been a Guide.

PART IV

Often, in ships at sea,
It has been sailor's fortune to behold
Icebergs, or hells of breakers, dead to lee,
And heard (upon the sight) a death-bell tolled.
And then, as ruin was at point to be,
Some sudden wind-shift has made Morning gold.

Again, at sea, how many times have men
Received, as Fate decreed,
Prompting, from wisdom beyond mortal ken,
To alter course, however mad the deed!
Yet altered course, though doubtingly, and then
Sighted and rescued folk in direst need.

Again, our elder seamen told a tale
About a ship astray with fires dead,
Her shaft gone in the gale,

With half her boats and half her manhood fled,
Herself engulfed with billow-battered rail
Driving on granite crags in surf ahead.

Yet, even as the appalling billows spouted
Their cataracts along her to the rock,
When death was due next minute as none doubted
And men braced to the shock;
There, at the roaring jaggings iron-snouted
Destiny bade the snapping jaws unlock.

Below them, in the milk of shattered sea,
Some unsuspected swirl of tidal race
Let not the crashing on the granite be
But swung the helpless steamer from the place,
From death and danger free
Though drenched by every breaker at the base.

Were not these Mornings bringing in the Spring,
That in some deathless city of Man's Aid
Have, from the joy, made happy bells to ring,
And left all hearing spirits less afraid,
And given to all thought a lifting wing,
Flags to Life's cavalcade?

PART V

Destiny orders much,
Opens or shuts her grim or golden gates,
Brings a Saint George to loose the dragon's clutch,

Warns the lost pilgrim where the tiger waits,
But within Man, here limping on his crutch,
Are unsuspected strengths that alter fates.

Sometimes, however seldom, comes the gift
The cloud dissolves . . . The True
Illumines all things as the shadows shift,
Changing the old into the startling new.
Man sways aloft, wind-balanced like the swift
Surveying all creation from the blue.

Then he perceives the majesties ordained,
Cleansed of misunderstandings, hates and lies:
The prisoner is unchained,
Out of the dewy grass the larks arise,
Beneath his Tree the seeker has attained;
In sunlight, in the singing, he is wise.

O secret little soul of suffering Man,
O spark (or comet) hidden in the cloud,
Thy light has made the dawn since Life began,
Has burned away the shroud,
Has shown a path, has hinted at a plan,
And left Life consecrated and endowed.

O dying Man, whose seeking has made known
The deathlessnesses round us that abide,
Whose being springs from harvests long since sown,
Whose hope is from the hopeful who have died,
Whose strength stands as the stone
From stalwarts perished, against Time and Tide,

Through thee we know that when Night threatens all,
When dragons of mis-doing bar the way,
When Night, and creatures of the Night, appal
And footing fails and devilries dismay,
Life, greater than Mankind's, is within call,
And, called to, will obey.

A STORM

South, in the Caribbean Sea, a haze
Of tropic heat sweltered through summer days.
The wilderness of water lapsed and hove
In brassy masses that the sharks' fins clove;
Aloft, in glare, a furnace seemed to brood
Unbearably in blinding solitude.

All was as listless, leapless, as when first
The smoking wrappings of the planet burst
And sunlight, for the first time, lit the show.

There is no now in anything below,
All aught is alteration into change.
The strangeness was already more than strange;
Hot, moistened air was rising from the sea,
A cooler air was where it used to be,
The air within a space was pressing less,
There was a movement in the listlessness;
An eddying about a heart began,
As Love (or other Frenzy) within Man.

Often in tropic calm the seaman sees
Blacknesses, water-spouts and vortices;
These (with the mirage) are the daily shows,
None (like a boy) a peril till it grows;

But this one grew and, travelling, became
(And soon) a threat to shipping, with a Name.

Those who beheld its birth saw but a squall.
A black sea rose, a black sky seemed to fall.
The blackness, darting lightning, spread and spread;
And silence fell and all the air was dead.
A sullenness in Nature numbed the brain,
It fretted flesh till old wounds ached again,
Till wry nerves jangled with the living sense
Of evil threatening man's impotence.
Terrified seabirds wandered in a daze,
Above the black were clouds like bloodied sprays.
All was unuttered, unutterable threat.
Whose sands were run? Whose destinies were set?

The Weather Station's warning said: 'A storm . . .
'(At such a point) is forming, or will form . . .'
Later: 'The mentioned system has increased
'Well marked, 'twixt here and there, and moving East.'

Eastward it thrust its gyratory rage,
This roaring devil with a war to wage;
Indrafts of wind-draught were its being's bread,
Far from it flew its menace to strike dead.
It sucked its being into wider space
Wherever weaker systems would give place,
Then, at a stronger system, paused, and tried
This way and that to make the bar divide.
Then swung north-westward, having found or made
A pass of air unguarded against raid.

Before its front, the Spanish Islands rose
Into blue peaks for ever capped with snows,
Scored by great gleaming cataracts that drowse,
Down the untrodden crags where eagles house.
Below, old forest; lower still, the plain
Sweet with all citrus fruit and sugar-cane,
So fragrant all, that sailors, far at sea,
Dream, as they sail, their ship nears Araby.

Most happy seemed those islands of delight,
The red-tiled farms, the tiny townships white,
The harbour gay with little flags and sails,
The pier-end piled with fruitage for the mails,

And everywhere the negroes in their joy
Taking delight in song in their employ.
Nearer these isles of Saints the cyclone drew;
Slowly occlusions blotted out the blue;
Something that was not smoke, nor mist nor cloud,
Passed on to light and living like a shroud.

Then, from the evil, mizzling rain that fell,
Nulled at the piers the slapping of the swell,
Then slowly worsened to a roaring rain
As though Earth never should know drought again.
Then in the rain, the wind, the roar, the force
Of all Earth's rage on all Earth's maddened horse,
Rain, lifting sea and tempest that destroyed
All that Man did, hoped, stored; and left it void.

Slowly, the cyclone whirled its vast ellipse,
Smiting the islands' fortune to eclipse,

Leaving the roofless walls to splinters blown,
The torrents washing cane-fields to the stone;
The pier a wreck, an island-schooner thrust
Into a church in some outrageous gust,
The iron sides of some lost steamer bent
Double and jagged where the dancing went,
Men buried in the cellars, and men gone,
All beasts destroyed . . .
The fury hurried on.

North-westward still its whirl of wreckage loose;
Its outer feelers threatened the sea-shore,
The eastern sea shore, of the Southern States;
Its outer fringes tattered at the gates,
But here the stablished Southern Summer stood.
The cyclone failed but shattered what it could,
And to the wide Atlantic bore away
Eastward, north-eastward, roaring for its prey.
And many a schooner sank, and many a ship,
Saved by her lucky oil-bags' steady drip,
Came limping into harbour all forlorn,
Her boats in matchwood and her bulwarks torn,
Her cargo shifted and her smokestack white
From drying spray, as tokens of the fight.
But one, the *Water's Queen*, arrived no more.

That wandering Queen, the last and fairest she
Of these foam-scattering prides that used to be,
She, homeward-bound, for Falmouth, as of old,
Knew well the weather that the signs foretold:

The strange and ghastly light, the evil sky;
The worsening rain-squalls never passing by;
The blackness with the hellish fiery streaks,
Th' increasing wind-roar rising into shrieks,
The snapping nerves, the mercury depresst,
The swell of sea from somewhere south and west,
The sheet-blocks hammering the masts: the wet
Spouting through ports, like devils giving threat
Before such fury of advancing gale,
All hands at eight-bells, midday, shortened sail.

She had endured all weathers hitherto,
The Horn, the Plate, the China Seas, she knew;
This, just the Western Ocean once again,
Though it might test, would but confirm her reign.
Still, it was dirty and approaching fast;
Her sails were furled and double gaskets passed.
Hove-to, beneath a weather-cloth, she rode.
The wind-whipped spray was white as if it snowed;
She rolled and shipped it green, and none knew well
If it were rain or snow or spume that fell.
But all the welkin screamed like nether hell.

Somewhere within that roaring anger's lust,
The powers raging focussed in a gust,
Something out-shrieking aught yet ever heard,
Out-blasting any rage, yet tempest-spurred,
Rage shotted blind with horizontal rain
That sliced the sea-tops level like a plane.

This tropic fury smote her with its blast:
The *Water Queen's* worst instant and her last.

Over she heeled before that thrust of Fate,
Within her thundered tons of shifting freight;
Down crashed her yards, blocks, chains, from overhead
Some strove to clear the boats: others were dead:
Some, for an instant, felt that she might rise,
Then bitter brine was pricking in their eyes
And water quenched the battle in their throats.
A last axe hacked at tackling in the boats,
Then, down she went into the secret slime
Of untold living that has had its time.

Leaving alive in that appalling sea
One leaky boat manned by a bleeding three.

On, on, blinding the sea, the cyclone sped.
Its lust of indraft all the welkin fed;
Its wandering fury seemed to have the mind
Of howling hounds intent to kill the find
Till lo, ahead, another storm as great,
Another force to merge with as a mate.
In mid-Atlantic, blotting sea and sun,
The centres merge, the hurricane is one,
One in its drive, its savagery, its force,
To overwhelm all purpose on its course;
To smite all ships, fish, birds, upon its way
Across a thousand miles of disarray.

Its toll of death is written in no book.
None knows, nor ever will, the toll it took,

But through the western world the daily press
Told the storm's progress and its hellishness.

And nearer to, for days, what did it seem?
Force in its utmost horror of extreme.
A thousand miles of grayness under gray,
Topped by a flying scud of rain and spray,
The league-long combers, marching from their crests,
Rage, crying 'Come' to Death and Doom as guests,
Sunlight and Joy and Beauty put away
Night after night, and then, day after day,
A roaring grayness under flying gray.

Westwards, towards the hurricane's abyss,
Adventured on the liner *Artemis*.

Great, beautiful and swift her splendour strolled,
Queen, like the star in Ephesus of old,
Ship of such wonder that she surely vied,
With aught from Boston, Belfast or the Clyde.

Warning in plenty came from sea and air
To all her seamen bidding them beware.
They saw the glass fall and the wind increase,
The swell break billow, putting end to peace.
The certainty was sure in every man
They faced the worst the North Atlantic can;
All about decks was double-lashed and chocked,
All port-holes levered tight, the oil-drips stocked.
The decks were snugged; below was not so well;
The ship was sure, less happy the hotel.

There, as she strode, her rolling plunges sent
All without handhold flying as they went;
From chests of drawers, drawers, at the roll,
Came joggling out to jamb, or spill the whole.
Chairs, tables, palm-pots slithered side to side,
The racing screw-blades jarred her in her stride.

In her saloon, her dinner tables stood:
With stewards more than diners seeking food ...
Sometimes, in plunges, down went dish and lid,
Knives, forks and diners into scuppers slid,
Once, twice, and thrice the men and crockage glid;
The brooms and buckets gathered up the mess.

Men cheered the sea-sick: 'This'll soon be less.'

Lifelines were stretched across to save men's bones,
All the vast fabric whined and uttered groans.
Above the thunder numbing shocks would tell
How tons of billow flooded either well.
Then at a sudden lunge a darkness burst
Lashing all port-holes as a side immerst.
Slowly she strode, yet still a little sped
Upon her course; dead slow, she went ahead.

Then, towards night, those on her bridge beheld
A rival Queen, another liner, quelled:
Her engines stopped, for safety lying-to,
While ever, over her, the spindrift flew.
The covers of her boats made tattered flags;
Her scuppers seethed; the oil dripped from her bags.

Laying her broadside down to ship it gray,
The vision faded in the dying day.

'Hove-to', a seaman said; and, as he spoke,
A billow, toppling up before it broke,
Still toppling up, approached, a moving mound,
A running hill coming from pits profound
All the Eight Miles of Malvern as it seemed,
Arising sepulchres of sea that gleamed.
Then darkness came, then pausing, then a roar
Such as no seaman there had heard before.

Then, instantly, the ship was one with sea,
Stunned into naught for an eternity . . .

A few cries came, with crash of smashing gear,
A wash, then a suspense, too great for fear,
Then more suspense, then slowly, from the grave,
The *Artemis* arose out of the wave,
Spouting, but living, with her boats in wreck,
And every scupper brimmed on every deck.
She rose; her seamen, underneath their feet,
Felt once again the engine's steady beat.

'That was a Ninth', her Captain said, and grinned.
And as he spoke, there came an end to wind;
The roaring ceased: the Centre come at last:
Centre, with promise of a stronger blast,
A waste of billows tumbling into spume,
Each confused heap an undirected doom.

A naught of welter after all the roar,
The brainless nothing that had made the war,
The voiceless nothing that had made the cry,
This nullity beneath a yellow sky,
Or yellow glare, crossed flittingly by wings
I' the hellish hurry of inhuman things.

But little space they passed, considering this.
From the south-west all ocean seemed to hiss,
Changing all else to cataracts of rain;
A moment's prelude to the roar again.
From an opposing point the tempest blew.
Watch after watch, the liner struggled through.
Her Master bade them, 'Keep her as she goes . . .
'Maintain the oil and call me when it snows.'

'Snow on the glass to starboard, now,' said one.

Snow, in good sooth, the cyclone's fringe, was won.

Within the bridge the arctic current struck,
The spindrift, smiting iron, froze and stuck.
Under the beacon of the mast-head light
The forward deck took icing and grew white.
'Blowing as hard as ever,' said the Chief,
'But before daylight there'll be some relief.
'We've had our penn'orth and we part as friends.'

Eastward the storm drove to the ocean's ends,
Breaking the billioned bubbles of its foam
On listed steamers struggling to reach home.

The bones of ships from Start to Finisterre
Trembled deep down within the conger's lair;
The Bishops seemed a planet set in spray;
Boats broke to matchwood within Falmouth Bay.

But now the cyclone found a barrier set.
South of the River Thames its match was met.

Strengths of high pressure centred over France,
Edging to westward, broke its wild advance.
It broke in rage, in welterings of rain.

On Berkshire chalk, in many a downland lane,
In spoil of unripe apples on the grass,
In gleams of sun, men saw the menace pass.
The sun prevailed; it shone; the showers ceased.
Wickham and Kelmscot weathercocks turned east.

LINES FOR THE RACE OF SAILING SHIPS LISBON TO THE HUDSON BRIDGE, NEAR MANHATTAN, 1964

Once, they were Queens, triumphant everywhere,
In every port their countless house-flags flew;
Wherever wind blew billows they were there
Smashing their shadows as they thrusted through.
All the world's commerce was their occupation,
Men cheered them going forth and entering in,
Each venture showed another crown to win.

I, who beheld them in their pride of old,
Cannot forget their splendour as they came
Superb, out of the perils never told,
Hoisting their colours and the four-flag name,
And the cable-rattle of their exultation
As anchor fell ere anchor-watch was set;
Who that beheld such vision can forget?

Today, the few survivors show again
Their glory of man's triumph over force;
Over the tumult of the seas they strain
Against the westers battling out the course,
The world's great sailing ships in emulation,
Their seamen praying to be first to hail
A New York pilot-schooner under sail. . .

Soon they will reach into the wondrous Bay,
The harbour, Mannahatta, the world's pride;
There, be the racer's fortune what it may,
Glory and grace attend on every side;
The flags of the great ships of every nation;
The towering City shining in the sun;
And the dear quiet after effort done.

There, each in place, the contestants will moor
Beneath the Statue lightening the world . . .
Masters and mates and men will make all sure,
All square the mighty yards, all canvas furled.
Then, with three cheers, the seamen each in station
Will haul the colours down and hoist the lights
And beating bells begin the festal rites.

THE ISLE OF VOICES

As the voice bade, I went ashore alone.
Being ashore, the green ship sped away.
The island was a baldness of bare stone,
Scaled both by fire and frost.
All Nature there seemed savage hate or error.
Not lifeless quite, for in its nooks of terror,
The horned asp with his poison watched for prey.

I saw no other life as I advanced:
A gully with its boulders hedged me in,
And I was terrified, but yet entranced,
For from the very rocks,
A woman's voice unprompted began singing
An unknown tongue that sent the pity winging,
And set the gooseflesh stark upon my skin.

For, though the singer seemed in extreme woe,
No one was there: none answered when I spoke;
The unknown in a grief I could not know,
Broke into sobs and ceased...
I scrambled up that gully of old granite –
No grimmer den can be in any planet –
And then a man's voice into sorrow broke.

'Something of you I understand', I cried.
'You are a chieftain such as I who speak.

'And you lament a comrade who has died,
'Or loved horse stricken dead.
'I, Ossian, bid you welcome here beside me.
'Come to me in this rocky gut and guide me.'
The voice fell still: the gully rose up bleak.

'This is a place of ghosts, this gut of stones,'
I thought, 'where lost ones wander when they die.'
Brook boulders, and bleached driftwood white as bones,
Led me to open glen.
And here a noise of bag-pipe, drum and crowder
Rang in my ears; it wavered; it grew louder.
A mob seemed there, invisible to eye.

Although a mob, its burden was of grief:
I heard of women dead, of leaders lost,
Of April bud become November leaf,
Of hearts broken in two,
Of ruin prompting some heroic daring,
Of captains facing death and not despairing,
Of banners battle-hacked and tempest-tosst.

All stilled: I wandered on, until a Fair,
Unseen, yet loud with trumpetings and cries
And whinnying horses, seemed about me there:
Men selling sheep or cows;
Men singing songs of mockery and laughter
Or ribaldries with tumults coming after . . .
All youth, all manhood, and yet all unwise.

Yet wondrous, all, for, though I could not see,
I felt that hidden in that empty space

The heart of man had his eternity
Within his day's extremes.
And hearing it, I anguished to be helping
Amid that tumult, mockery and yelping
To bring a smile upon that unseen face.

Yet, as I listened, the good temper changed;
Disputes were there, a quarrelling began,
The furies made the mob like men deranged;
Then blows were struck, and rage
Ran in full frenzy with the rabble shrieking
From sick despair or maddest vengeance wreaking.
I heard the woe and agony of man.

Then presently all stilled: the mob was gone,
Forgotten as mobs are, save as a curse
Haunting the landscape, so I wondered on
Uphill again. Up hill;
Into the chasms, where the winds that chattered
Were saying, 'Nothing matters, nor has mattered.
'Nature is evil all, but Man is worse.'

'Curs ever yap,' I answered, and advanced
Up ancient glacier-channels towards peaks
Unclimbed, whereto no eagle ever chanced,
Nor any noise of man.
Far, far below I saw the ocean boundless;
Above, blue empty heaven, windless, soundless,
The loneliness for which the spirit seeks.

The Sun went down beyond that soundless sea,
The green west swiftly dimmed as darkness came.

Save for the rock-scraps dropping on the scree
In those high crags, all stilled.
In the intensity a planet brightened,
And all things shrank because the world was frightened,
And crouched at something there that has no name.

Then, suddenly, Might pressed upon my brow:
I understood what man can understand,
Eternity, as apprehended now,
In one lone instant's light.
The touch upon me twitched the veils asunder,
All wisdom in her beauty and her wonder
Was light to me and impulse to the hand.

I do not know how long the glory held,
I was within eternity a while:
Within the Lasting where the Deathless dwelled
In Truth none can impugn.
All was in utter light, nothing was hidden,
Nothing within such light could be forbidden,
Nothing could wither it, nothing defile.

Light slowly dawned upon the solitude;
No wind breathed, no bird sang, no crumble fell,
But Mind from everlasting seemed to brood
Alone there, with the sky.
I seemed to hear the rocks speak in the ranges:
'Mortal, endure the justice of the changes . . .
'*We* were once molten lava in a Hell.'

They ceased, but other voices then began:
'The Change that alters all may make amends . . .'

'You suffered changes ere becoming Man;
'Now you can sing of Spring.'
'In every earthly change is some amending.'
'Old gratefulnesses wait with their befriending.'
'The iron time seems endless, but it ends.'

Then, many voices uttered: 'Give; oh give.
'The joy of giving is a gift's return.'
'And any Death in you makes something live,
'And Life itself gives thanks.'
'A moment's gift wins some eternal pardon,
'A daisy more in an undying garden,
'A fetter snapped, a lesson less to learn.'

A silence fell: the Sun strode from the Sea,
I became conscious that a Presence stood,
Saying, 'All coming here may question me.'
None showed: but the voice spoke.
I asked, 'What profit has my living taught me?
'Have I been wise in battling with who fought me?'
The voice said, 'Men must make their footing good.'

I said: 'My Father, Finn, and I, were foes.
'My comrades, the Fianna, are all dead.
'My lovely Mother lost – where, no man knows –
'My Niamh sent me here.
'Her love is beyond price to me, the friendless.
'But who am I to have such riches endless?'
'The Justice has ordained it', the voice said.

'What is the effort of our two to be,
'In Eire, or the Country of the Young?'

'How high is Heaven? How deep is the sea?
'And Wisdom's bounds, how far?
'How many Kingdoms truly worth the winning
'Tempted your Father at a raid's beginning?
'How many songs has Ossian not yet sung?'

'I cannot tell,' I said; the voice replied:
'No . . . nor how utterly souls can be twinned.
'No . . . nor how cruelly the soul is tied
'To sympathy with Man.
'How Fortune links a being with a city
'To height of high emprise, to depth of pity.
'Nor whence the star falls, nor where goes the wind.

'Finn's fief in Eire calls; the Hooked Hill,
'Trostan all blithe with bees, the rain-bright glen,
'These stir you, and your kindred call you still,
'Though wisdom guards you close.
'And song is wisdom and the harps are tempting.
'What does your spirit yearn to be attempting?
'What restless dream? What misery of men?'

'I am but Man', I said, 'I cannot tell;
'Life, in itself, is glory to the brave . . .
'Once, on Coisnafon Beach I found a shell,
'Such as no man had seen.
'Somewhere, to south and westward, as I reckoned
'There is a strangeness, and the sunset beckoned
'To me, to seek it, though it brought a grave.

'But here, with Niamh, much I set aside.
'Age reckons much unworthy to be sought.

'And undiscovered marvels still abide
'Somewhere, though not yet known.
'Sometimes, at dead moon, when the skies are dimmer,
'Beyond all space a starness seems to glimmer. . . .
'New Suns, new moons, new stars, beyond all thought.'

'Ossian, since Life is greater than you think,
'Were it not fit that Captains such as you
'Should summon friends to press beyond the brink,
'To find truth face to face?
'To hear Queen Wisdom at her music playing
'New harmonies for unknown life's obeying
'Were it not joy to join such retinue?'

Then voices cried: 'Attempt . . . and make mistakes.
'While you are breathing man, draw lively breath . . .
'The nights are long, but yet the morning breaks
'And all the birds begin;
'The mill-stones of the wits are ever grinding.
'Brother, the yet unfound is worth the finding.
'Seek Beauty, Brother, for it out-lives Death.

'If all the tales are told, re-tell them, Brother.
'If few attend, let those who listen feel.
'Any brave effort will inspire another.
'You have all time to try.
'What though the sailing never bring you plunder,
'The sea vouchsafes you wonder after wonder
'And ever just is Fortune's turning wheel.'

The voices merged into the sea-gulls' mewing;
I wakened, then, to Niamh out at sea,

The green ship's mainsail tugging at the clewing,
Nearing our Shining Land.
I said, 'O Niamh, nothing is forbidden,
'Not even Peace, but all the doors are hidden
'And iron-locked, and we must find the key.'

KING GASPAR and HIS DREAM

I had not meant to utter to men's ears
The holy things from which my spirit bleeds,
But I have done with sorrow, and Death nears,
And (being old) none cares (if any heeds).
But in a dream the glory that was She
Shone in my spirit and enlightened me.

This was my dream: there was a monstrous sky
Thund'rous with storm before me as I stood,
And two gray granite towers, four-square, high,
Were right and left, unutterably good.
Upon their roofs were pyramids untold
Of Paradise's fruits all glowing gold.

The doors and windows of the towers were fast,
Shuttered and barred, no person went or came,
But brightness smote those towers like a blast
And lit the empurpled darkness with its flame:
So may a winter sunsetting illume
A pine wood upon downland from its gloom.

And She was there, illuminously bright
Clad as in sky, so jewel-studded o'er
That all her very presence shed a light
Such as no waking eye-ball ever bore.

It was Herself, returned out of her Star,
More beautiful than earthly women are.

O ecstasy of eyes; then to my ears
Nay, to my very spirit, came the tone,
The voice so silent for so many years,
The inmost voice that spoke to me alone:
'The morning comes', she said, 'the tempest thins.
'Our Night is ended and our day begins. . . .

'Now, to our souls, this Fortune comes to be
'That, within little space, as Time is told,
'It will be granted that you come with me
'To learn the wonders that these towers hold,
'To let in light, to open all the doors,
'To halls and stairs, to rooms and corridors.

'Many and evil prisons lie below,
'Things of old ill and murder in the night,
'With chains in rust from blood shed long ago,
'And broken tools from tortures of old spite.
'But these are gone, their roofs are fallen in,
'On paven ways our questings will begin.

'Unknown to us the untrodden stairs and ways,
'Unknown the darkness just beyond the bend,
'Unknown the thing behind the door that sways,
'Unknown the footsteps sensed as we ascend
'We cannot know what dreads or glories be
'Until we open, let in light, and see.

'The will is in ourselves, that will attempt;
'The keys are in ourselves that will unlock;
'The prize is all fulfilment of dream dreamt,
'Springs in Sahara, harvest amid rock,
'Treasure on treasure to the will that drives
'Despite of grief and hate through bitter lives.

'This is the venture that awaits us here,
'Exploring these two towers inly linked,
'Both truly one, not two, as they appear,
'But shadowed both till light make them distinct:
'Distinct as on the summit of each one
'Those pyramids of Apples of the Sun.

'We, the disunioned two, who have long known
'The soul's starvation, parted from a friend,
'The emptiness of being all alone,
'The daylong days, the nights that never end,
'Now have reward, inestimable gain
'Quest beyond price, with unity again.'

At this, her radiant beauty grew so bright,
The towers, with their pyramids, so glowed,
I could no longer see them for the light:
Light, and more light, through which no image showed;
The light that ended chaos, light that saves,
That brings the Spring and triumphs over graves.

Thus did she speak of happiness to be
Certainly, soon, ere many days were done,
Her very self at very one with me,

Impulse and purpose both at very one . . .
What more to say, but that I dearly wait
Commanding Death's tense whisper at the gate.

Here, then, I linger at my study fire,
About the lamp a moth is butting dim,
Without, the leaves fly at the wind's desire,
A tawny owl bewails the grief in him,
The quarter moon wests silver to the sea.
One hour more, and She will be with me.